Write your name.

Bee, Inky and Snake decide to go on a picnic. Inky is bringing yogurt. yummy yellow yogurt *y, y, y.*

Y y

Action: Pretend to be eating a yogurt and say *y, y, y.*

yummy yellow yogurt

y

y

yy

_ogurt

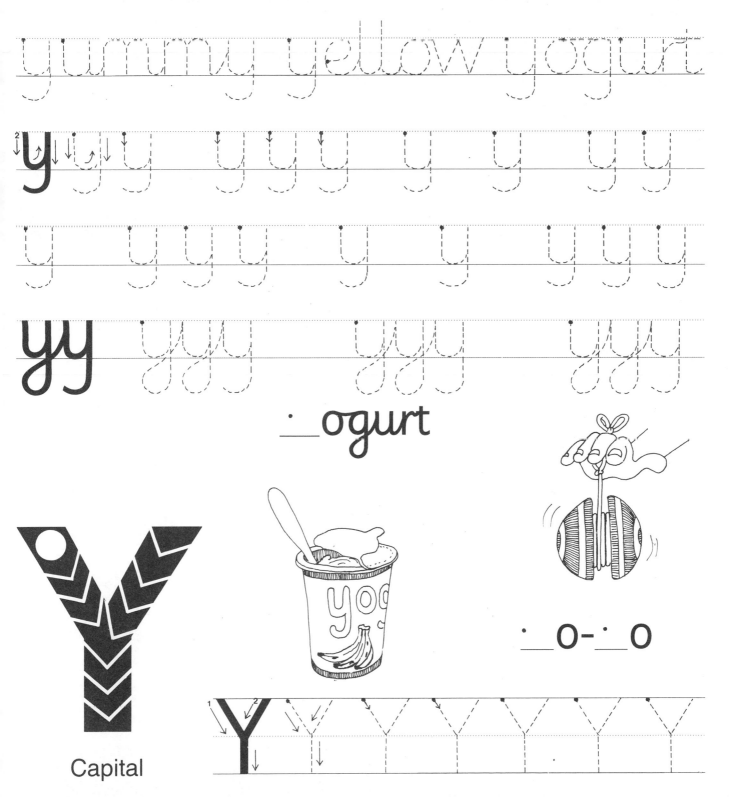

Capital

Y

_o-_o

3

X x

The girl has broken her arm.
Her brother is pretending to take an x-ray.
He points and goes *ks, ks, ks.*

Action: Pretend to take an x-ray with an x-ray camera, saying ks, ks, ks.

X borrows the sounds of k and s.

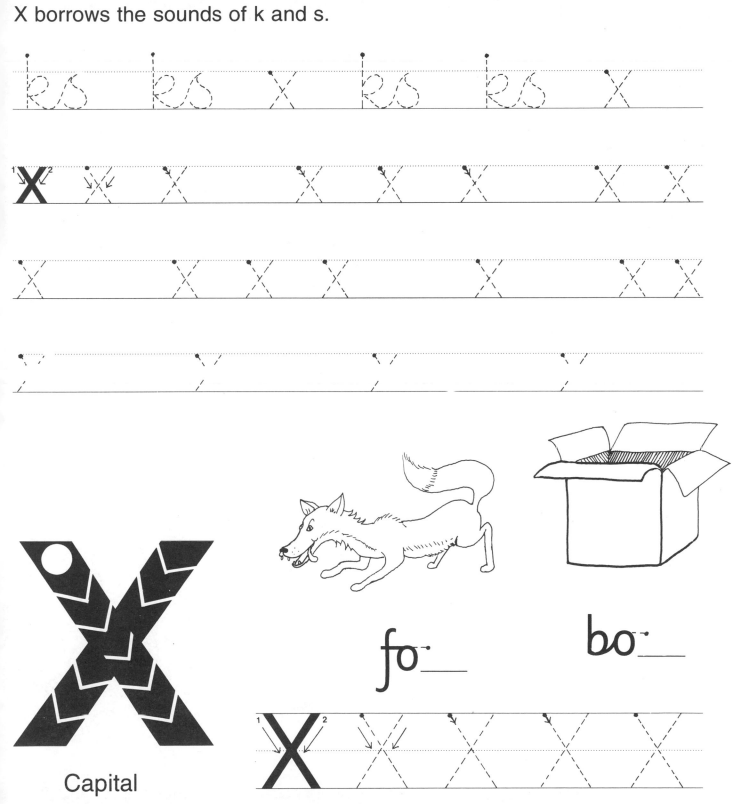

fo___

bo___

Capital

5

Bee, Inky and Snake have seen an old steam train.
They pretend that they are on it, going *ch, ch, ch.*

Action: Move arms at sides as if you are a train, saying *ch, ch, ch.*

Tall letters are joined about halfway up,
not at the top /\/\/\/ X or bottom ⊥⊥⊥⊥ X

ch ch ch ch

choo choo

ch ch ch ch

ch ch ch ch ch ch

ch ch ch ch ch ch

chch chch chch

__icken

__eese

bun__

sh

Everyone must be very quiet so the baby is not woken up.

Action: Place finger over lips and say *sh, sh, sh.*

Go up to where the next letter starts then write that letter in the ordinary way. Notice the difference to the letter s when written after a join.

ss   sss   sss   sss   ss

hush hush

sh   shsh   shshsh   sh

sh   shshsh   shshsh

sh   shshsh

fi___

___ell

___eep

To show the different sounds, th (as in this) and **th** (as in thick) are shown differently.

th

The clowns from the circus are very rude.

th

Action: Pretend to be naughty clowns and stick out tongue a little for *th,* and further for *th*.

Remember tall letters join about halfway up.

thin and thick

In writing an ordinary th is used.

th

th th th th th th

th th th th th th

th th th th th

fea__er   mo__   __ree

Alphabet

Write the capital letter next to the little letter.
Remember capital letters never join.

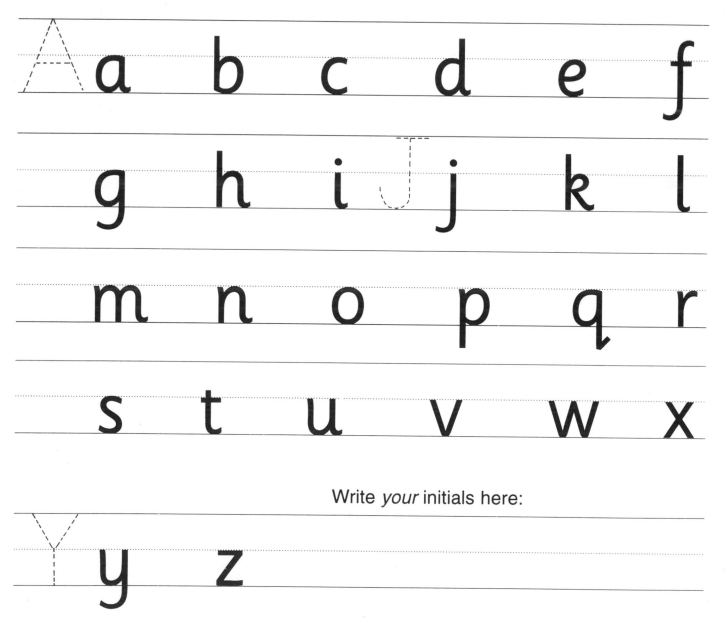

A a   b   c   d   e   f

g   h   i   j   k   l

m   n   o   p   q   r

s   t   u   v   w   x

Write *your* initials here:

Y y   z

Animal Anagrams

 t c a

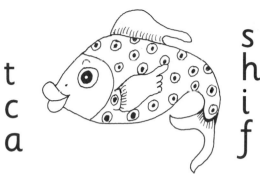 s h i f

 t o a g

 c a t

_ _ _ _

_ _ _ _

 t i b a r

 x o f

 r a c b

_ _ _ _ _

_ _ _

_ _ _ _

 l s a i n

 a r p o r t

 i c h e c k n

_ _ _ _ _

_ _ _ _ _ _

_ _ _ _ _ _ _

Consonant Blends

How quickly can you say them?

cr **tr** **br** **sn**

pl **fl** **gl** **cl** **st**

fr **sk** **sw** **sm** **sp**

spr **bl** **dr** **gr**

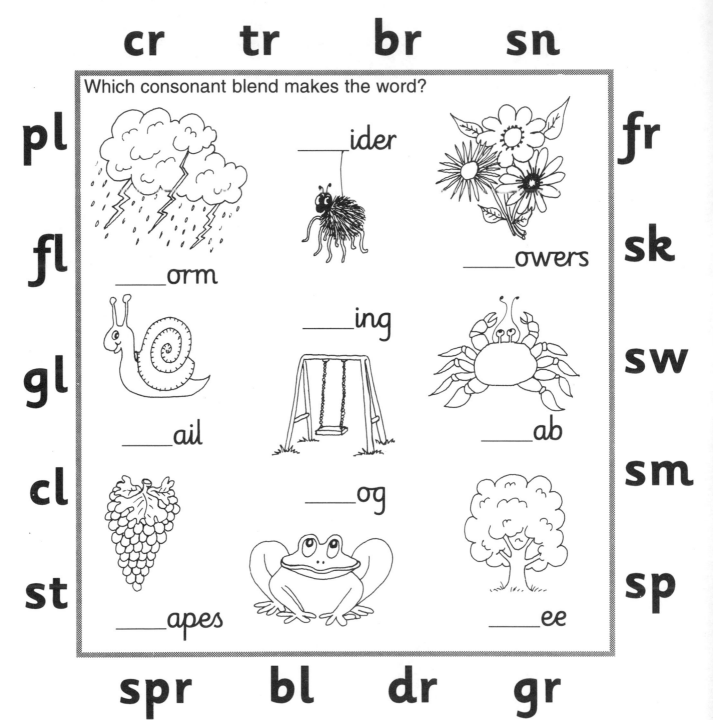

Which consonant blend makes the word?

____orm

____ider

____owers

____ail

____ing

____ab

____apes

____og

____ee

Write each word and read it. Then draw a picture of it.

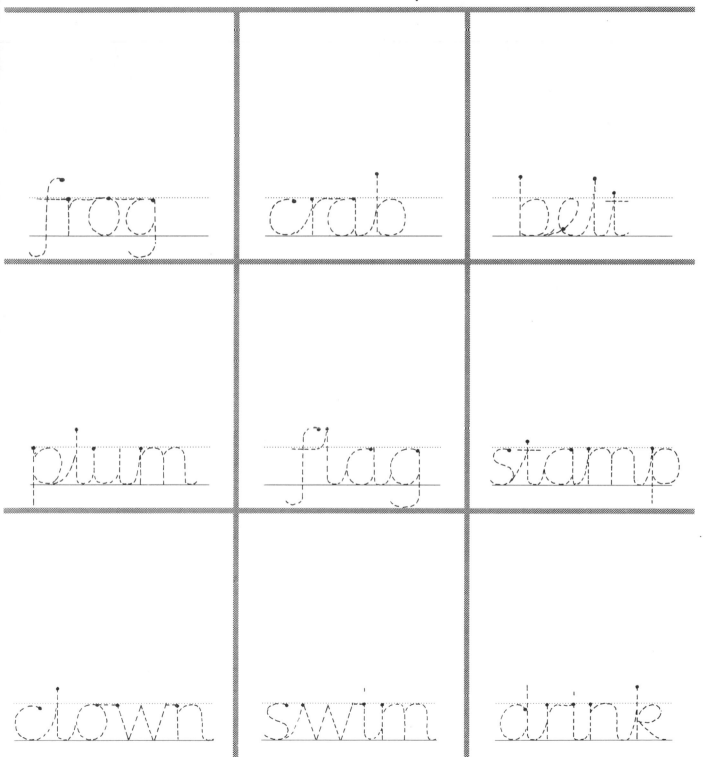

frog

crab

belt

plum

flag

stamp

clown

swim

drink

Say each picture, and write the sound to complete its name.

sh   **ch**   **th**

__eep   mo__   __ree

__eese   fea__er   __ark

__ick   __ell   __op

Say each picture, and choose the correct way to write it.

oa   **o_e**   **ow**

When joining m and n you must start at the top and go *down* first.

Put the scales on the dragons.

Is it true? Write Yes or No next to each one.

Fish can swim. _____

Dogs lay eggs. _____

Sheep can fly. _____

Rabbits can hop. _____

Parrots have wings. _____

Chickens chop wood. _____

Say each picture, and choose the correct way to write it.

ee   *ea*

Choose the correct sentence and write it under the picture.

A duck swims on the pond.
The dog is eating a bone.

The sheep are on the hills.
The chicks run to the nest.

T

Picture Sound Puzzles

Adding sounds.

p + 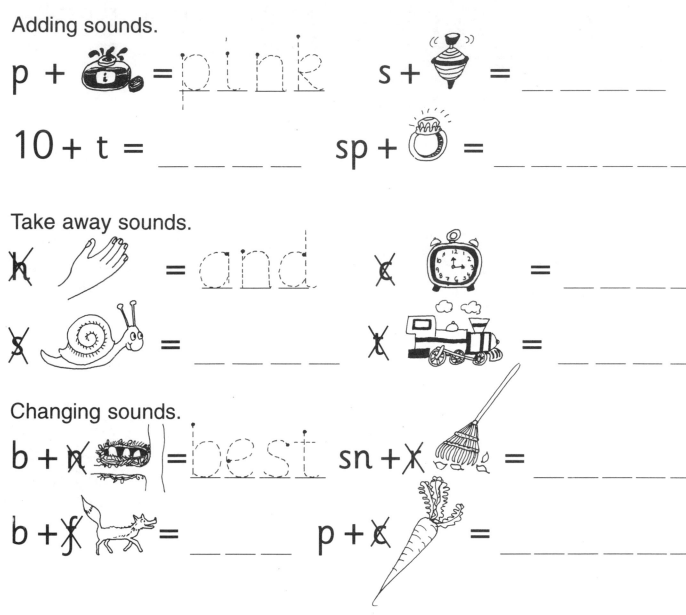 = pink   s + = _ _ _ _ _

10 + t = _ _ _ _ _   sp + = _ _ _ _ _ _

Take away sounds.

X = and   X = _ _ _ _

X = _ _ _ _ _   X = _ _ _ _ _

Changing sounds.

b + X = best   sn + X = _ _ _ _ _

b + X = _ _ _ _   p + X = _ _ _ _ _ _

Name Game

Try exchanging the first sound in your name.

Try using each letter of the alphabet.

The number 6.

1 2 3 4 5 6

Count the ladybirds.

6 6 6 6 6 6

Find the six ladybirds.

six six six six

Activity

X-ray Pictures

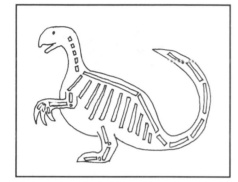

Cut out the shape of an animal from dark paper. Use white straws to make the animals bones.

Sheep

Use cotton wool and card to make some sheep.

Cut out the pieces from card. Paint the head and legs black. Stick pieces of cotton wool on the body, and a small piece on top of his head. Hang your sheep up, or make some more for a big picture.

th and th

Use two paper plates and make them into clowns faces by drawing on them or using sticky paper. Cut out a short tongue and a longer tongue from some pink paper and stick them on the clowns. Write th or th on the tongue. If you want you can make tongues that go in and out. Make a slit where the mouth is and make the tongue quite long. Slip the tongue through the slit, pull it in and out.